# This Coloring Book Belongs to:

That 25 Fun drawing pag-
es with numberd-zone about
wildlife animals for adults
and kids

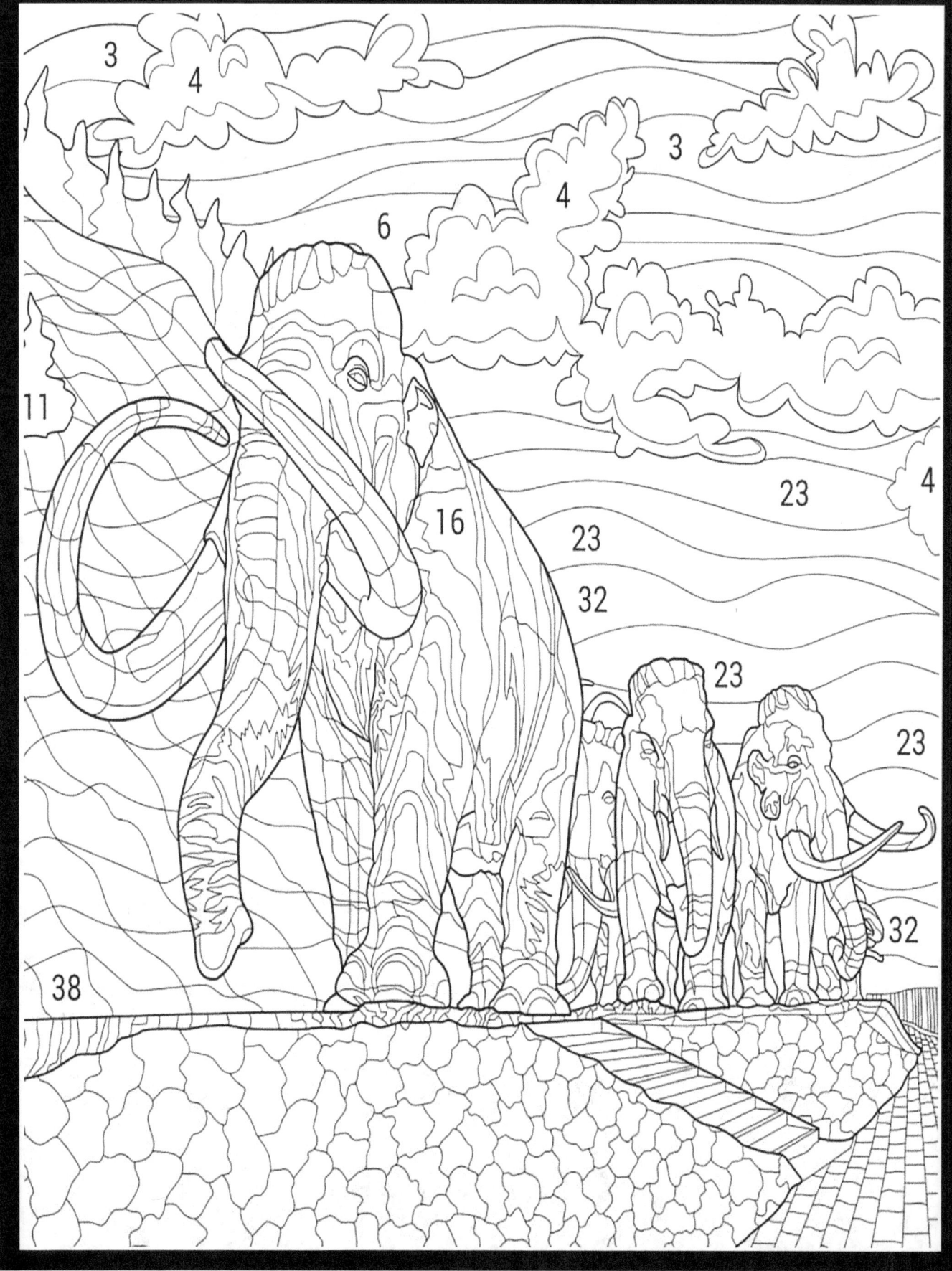

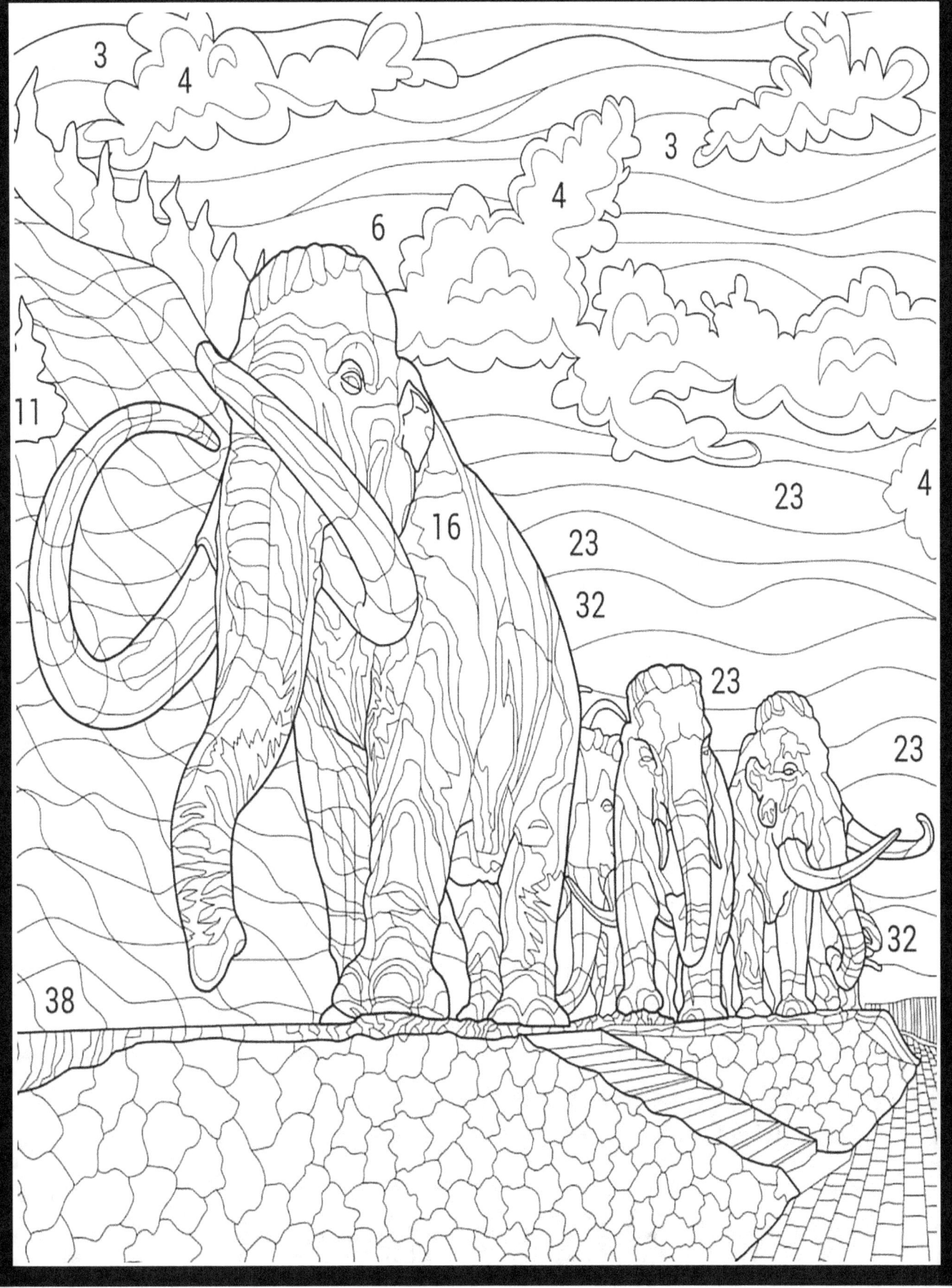

BIG TIGER

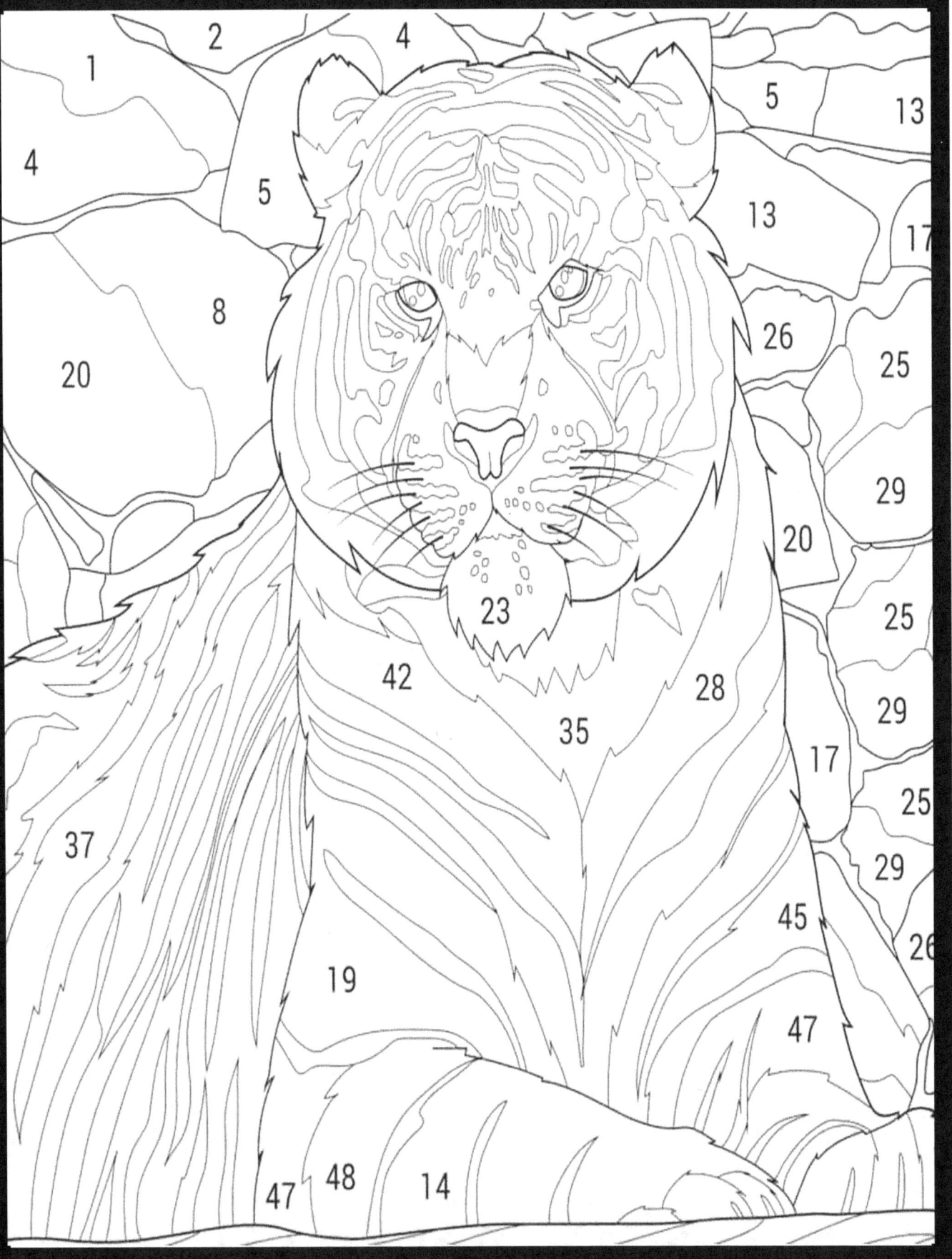

LONG GIRAFFE

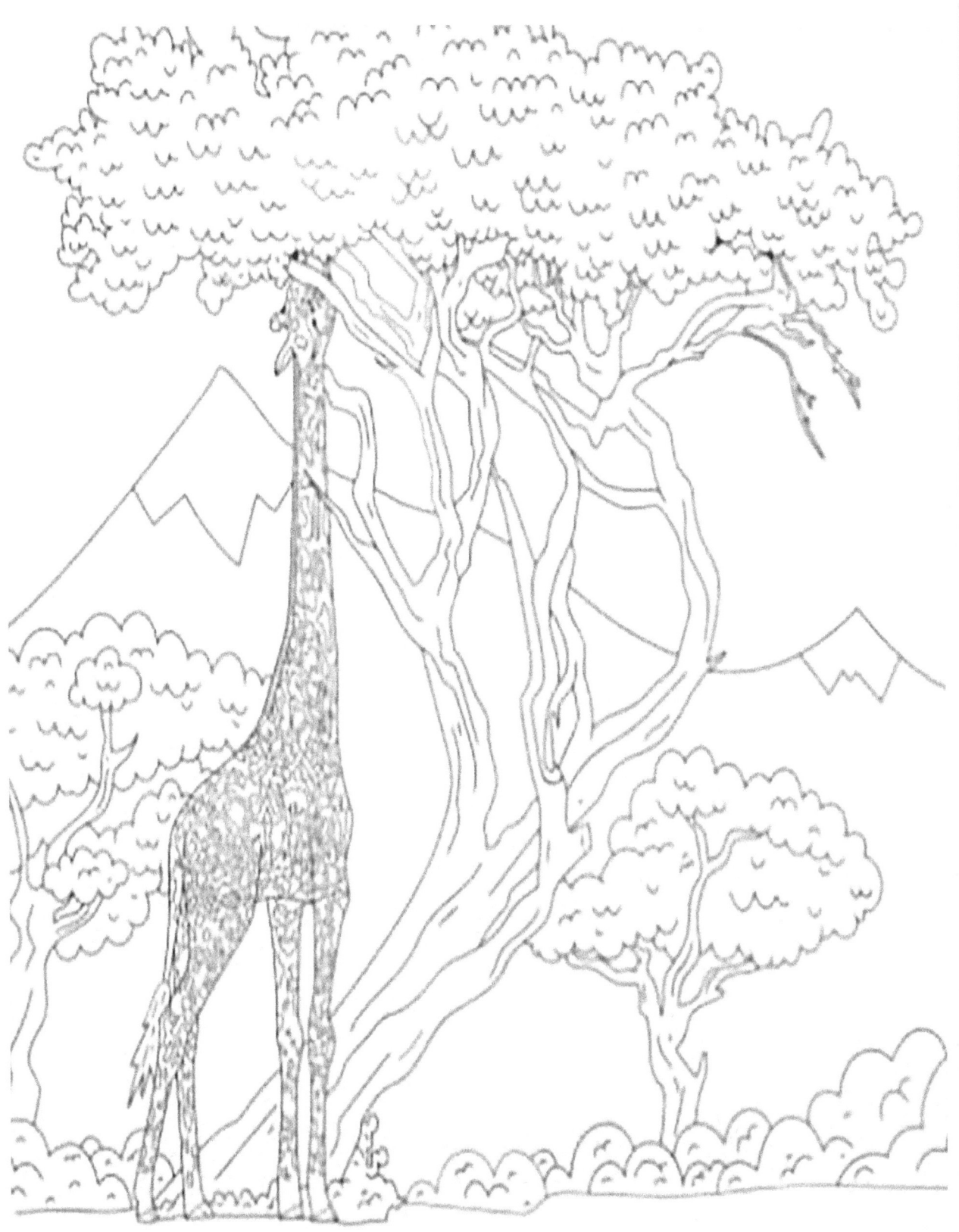

THIRSTY CHEETAH

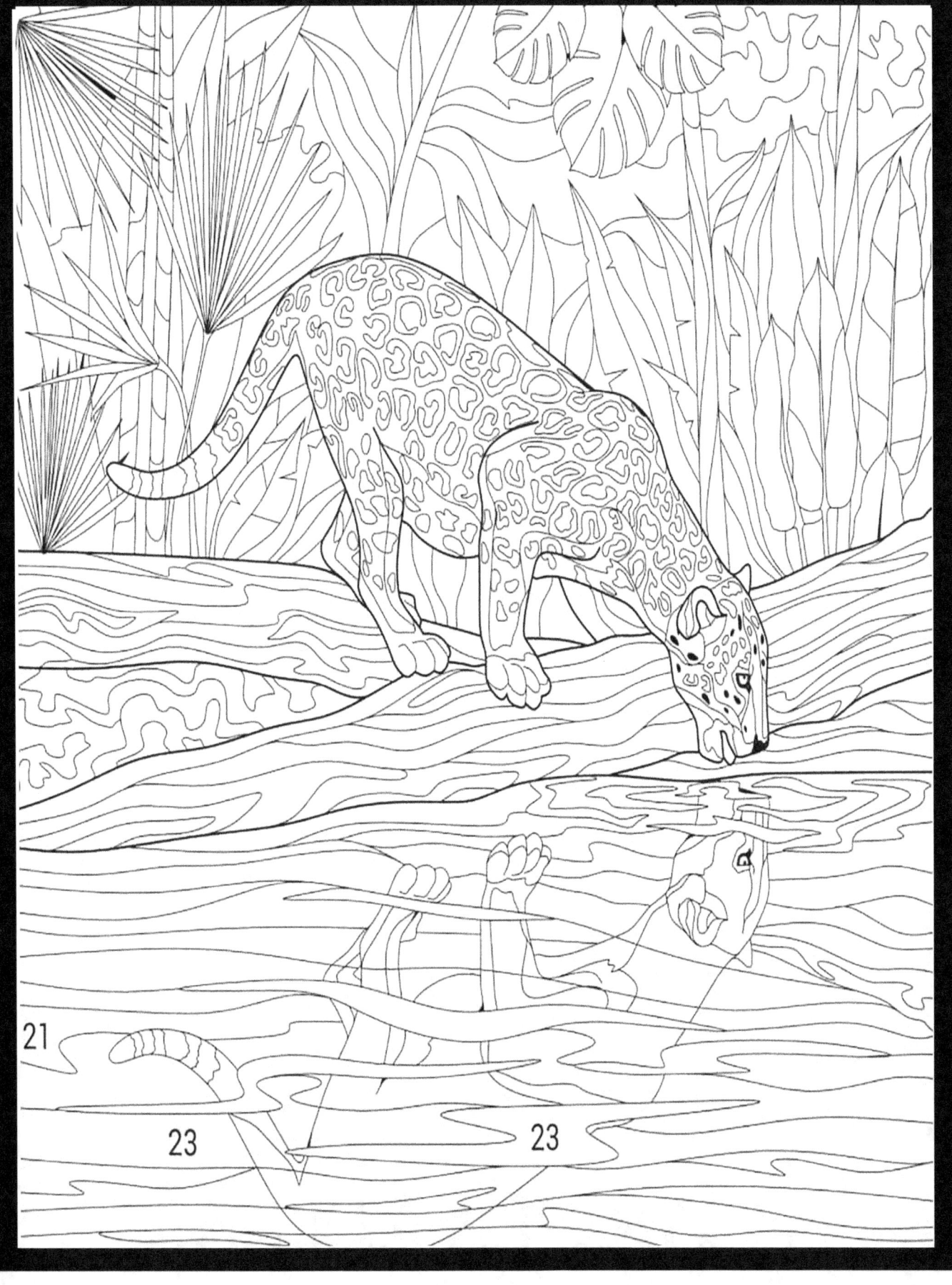

STRIPED ZEBRA

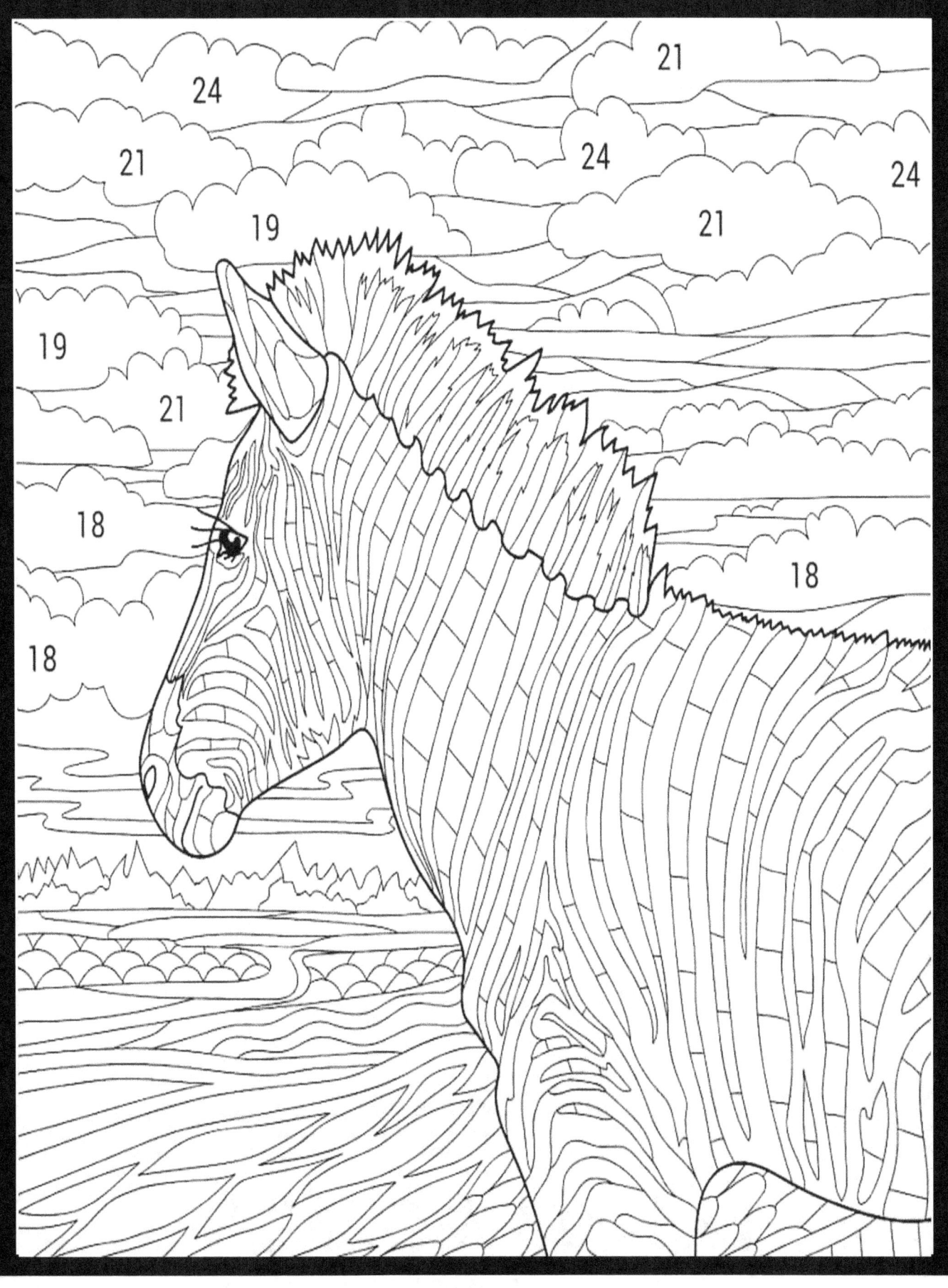

FUNNY MONKEY

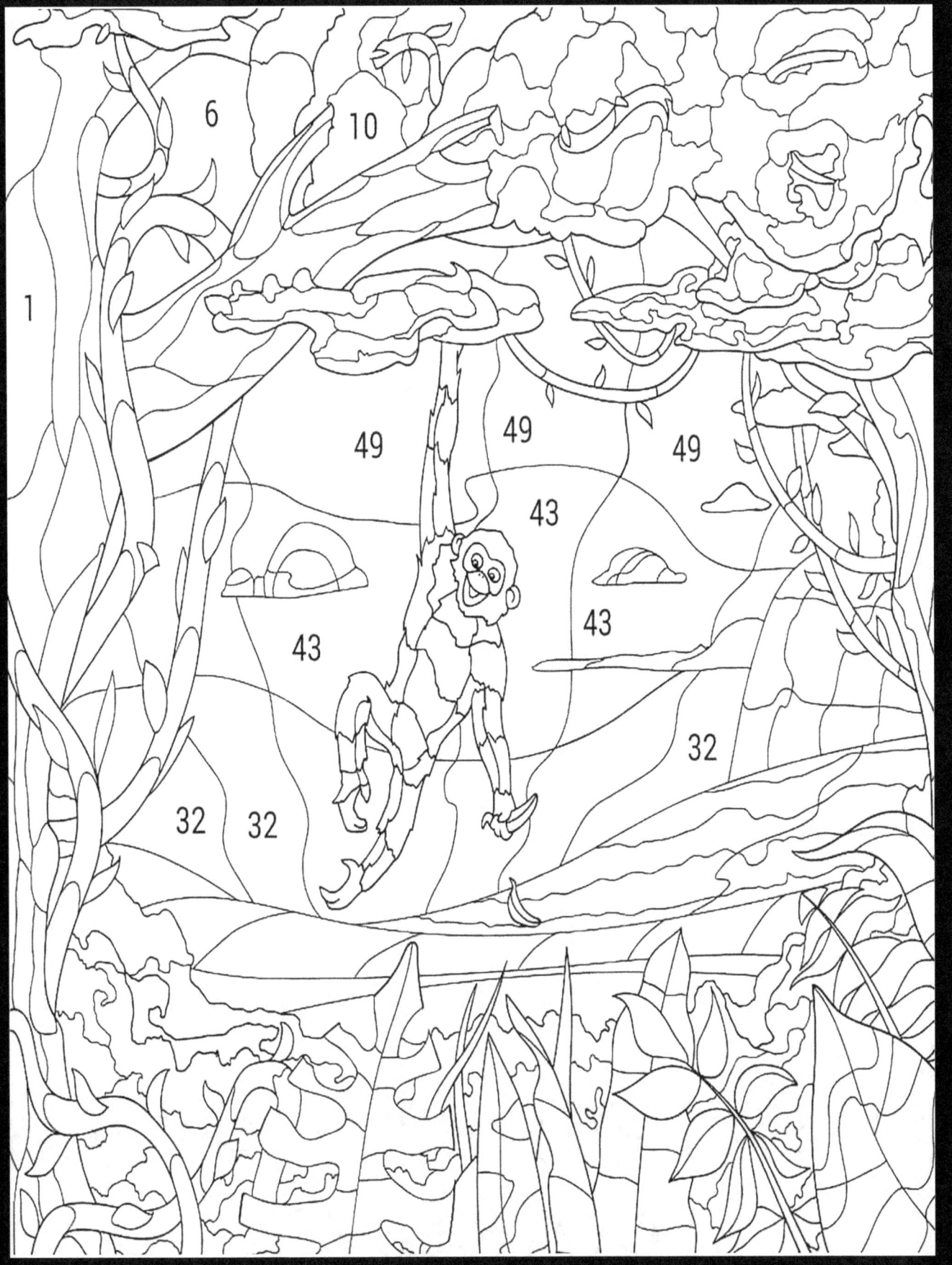

# WHAT THIS WILD ANIMAL FOOTPRINT?

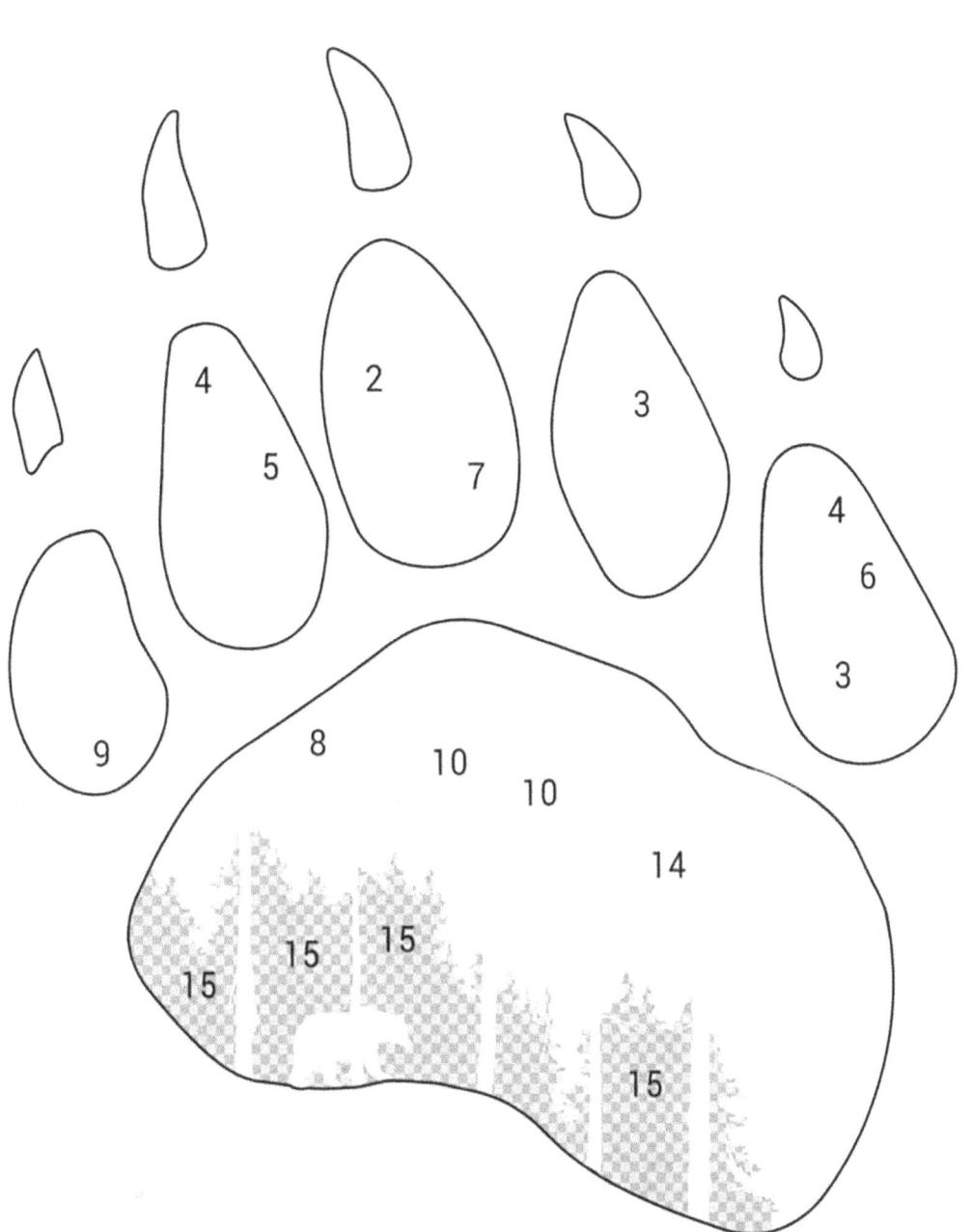

IM EXHAUTED DEER!!

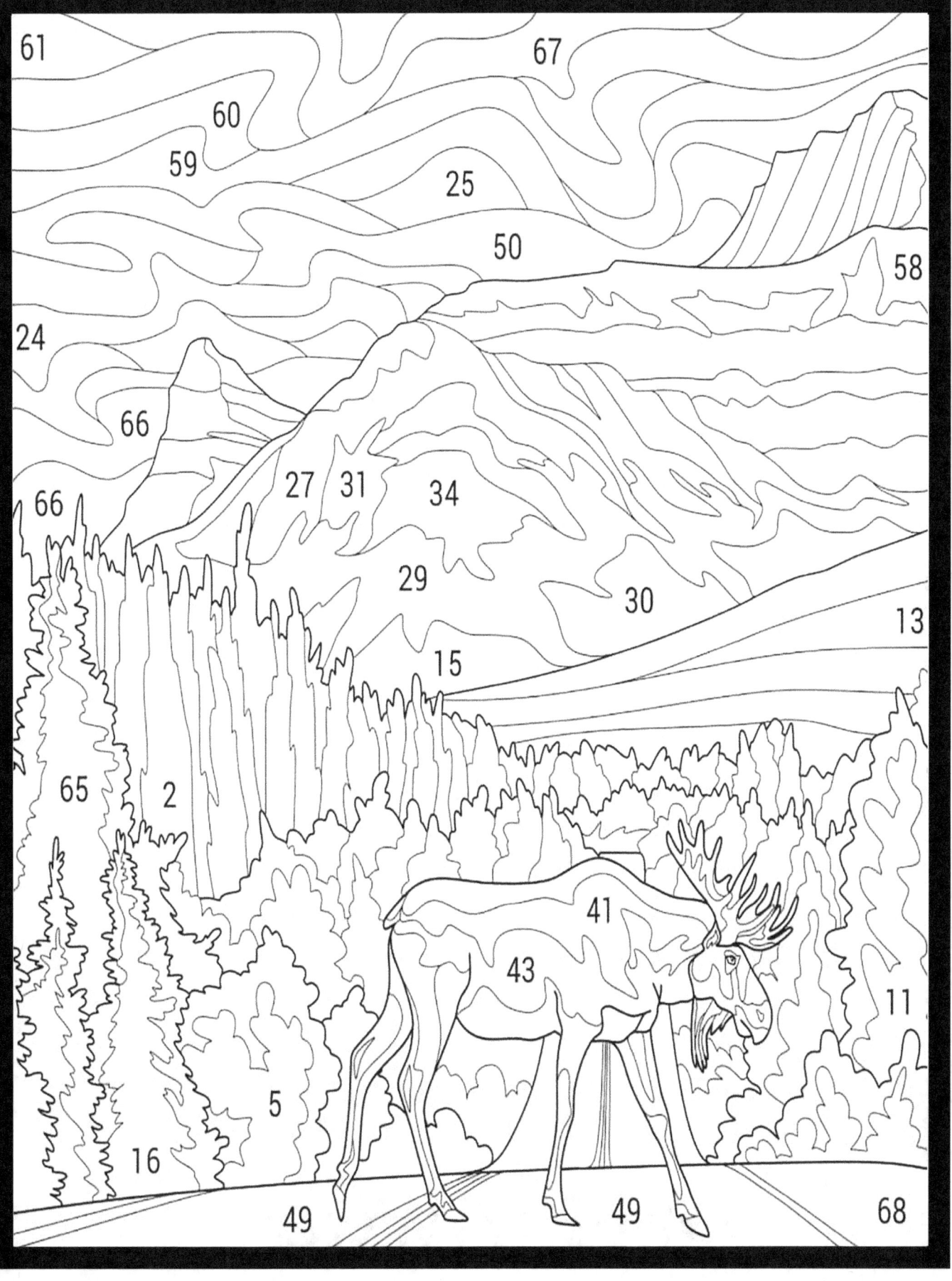

ANGRY WOLF

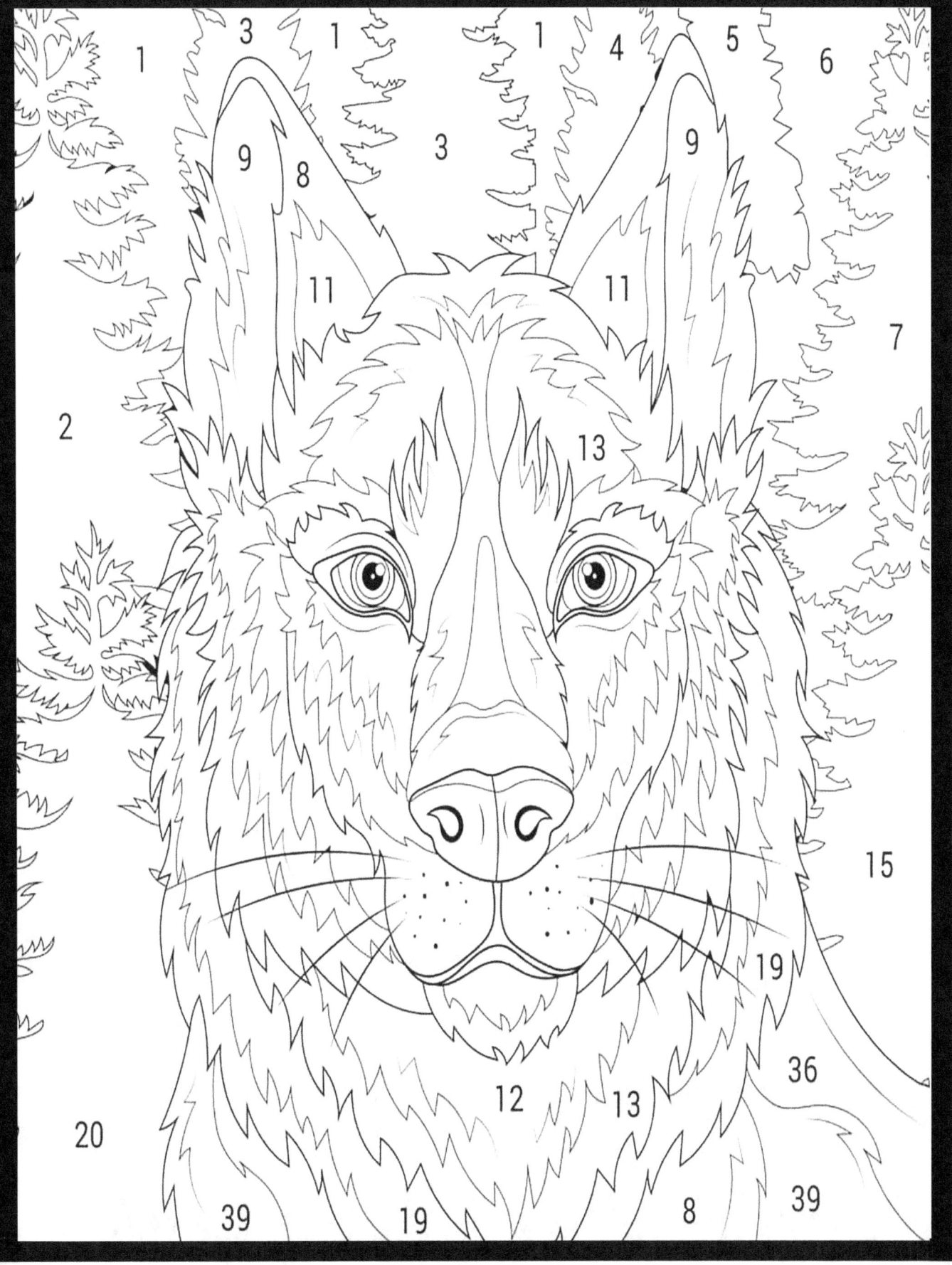

BEAUTIFUL WILD LAMB

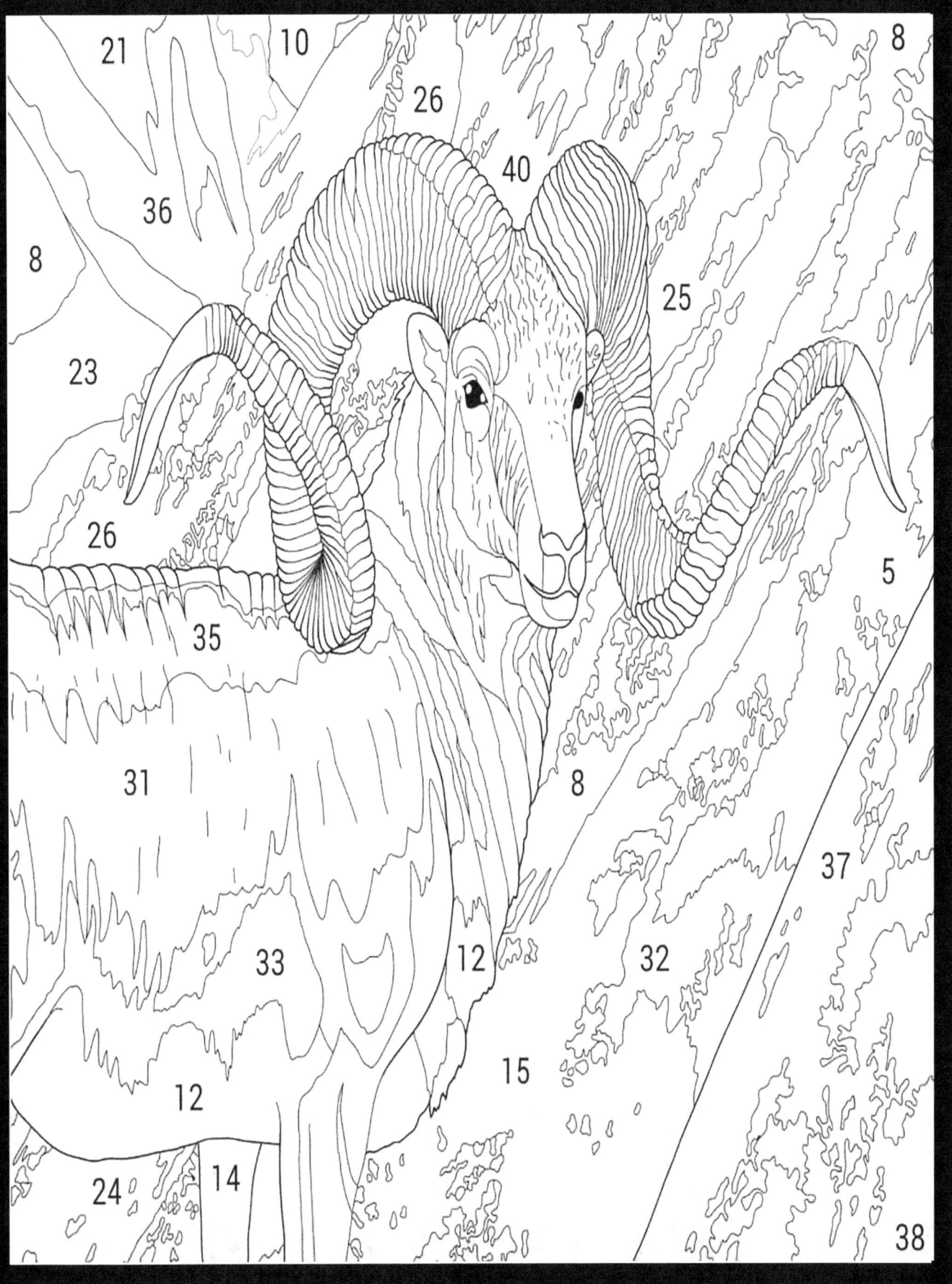

THE TRICKY FOX

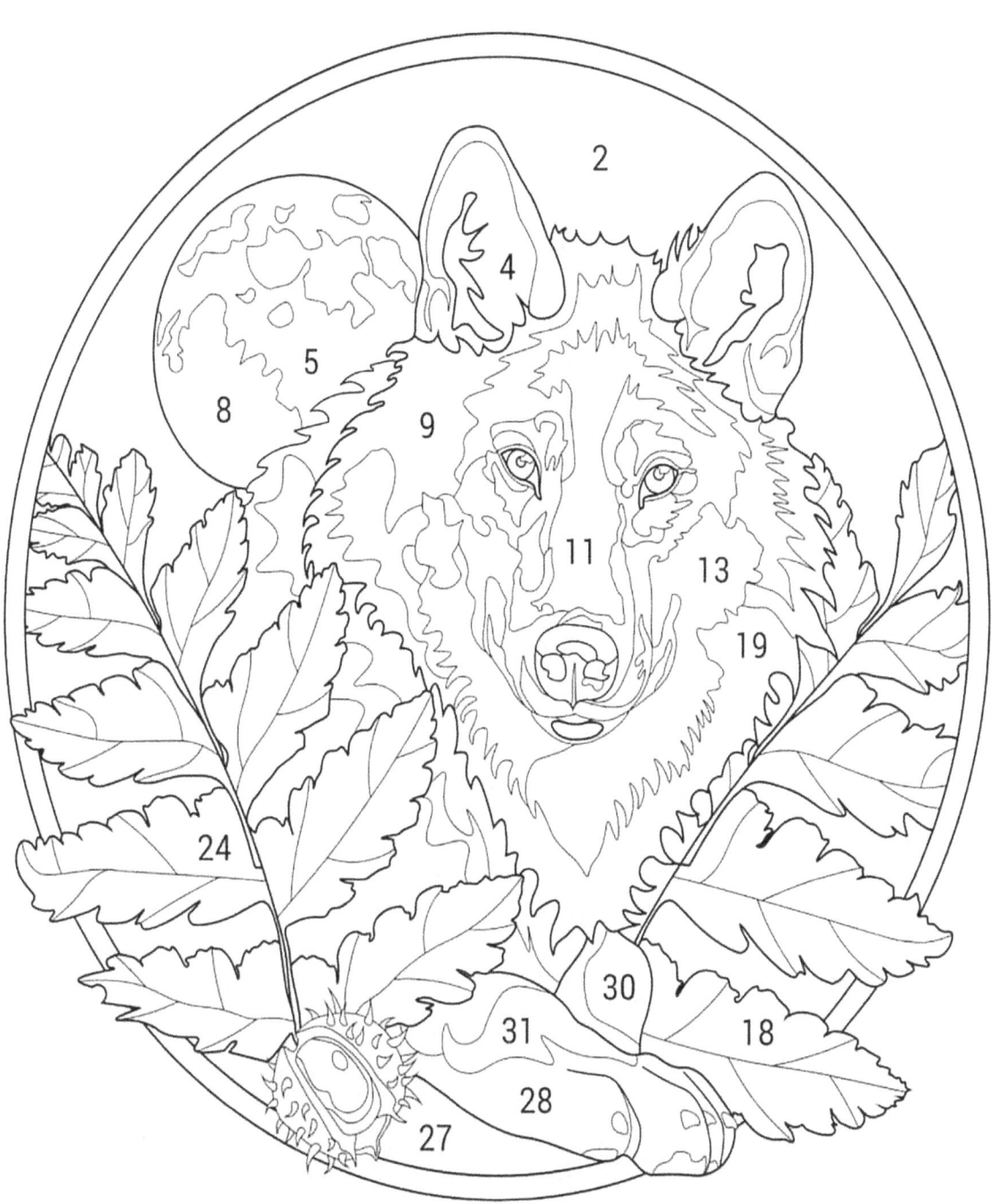

Red-Nosed Reindeer

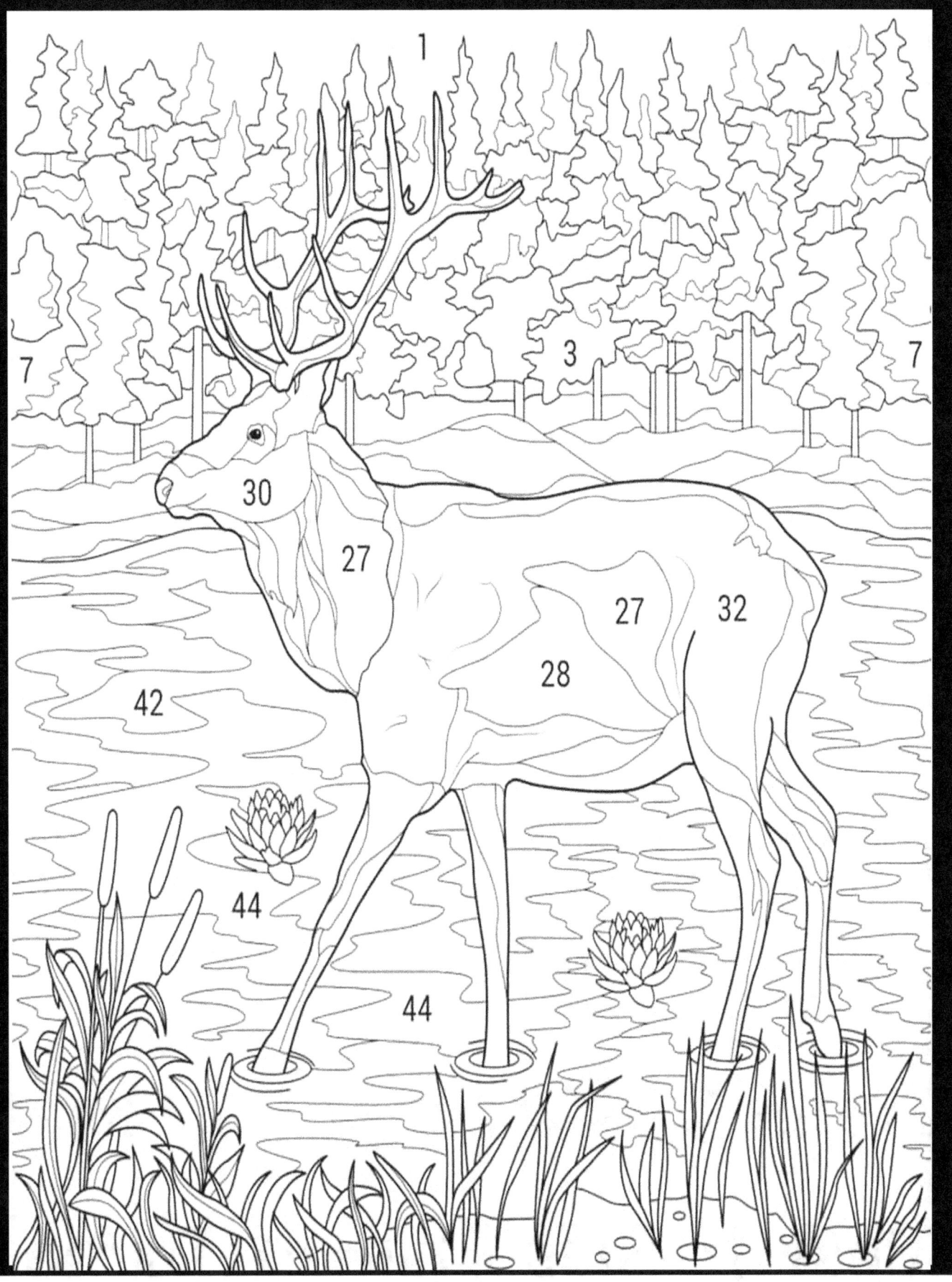

Best friends Rhino & Turtle

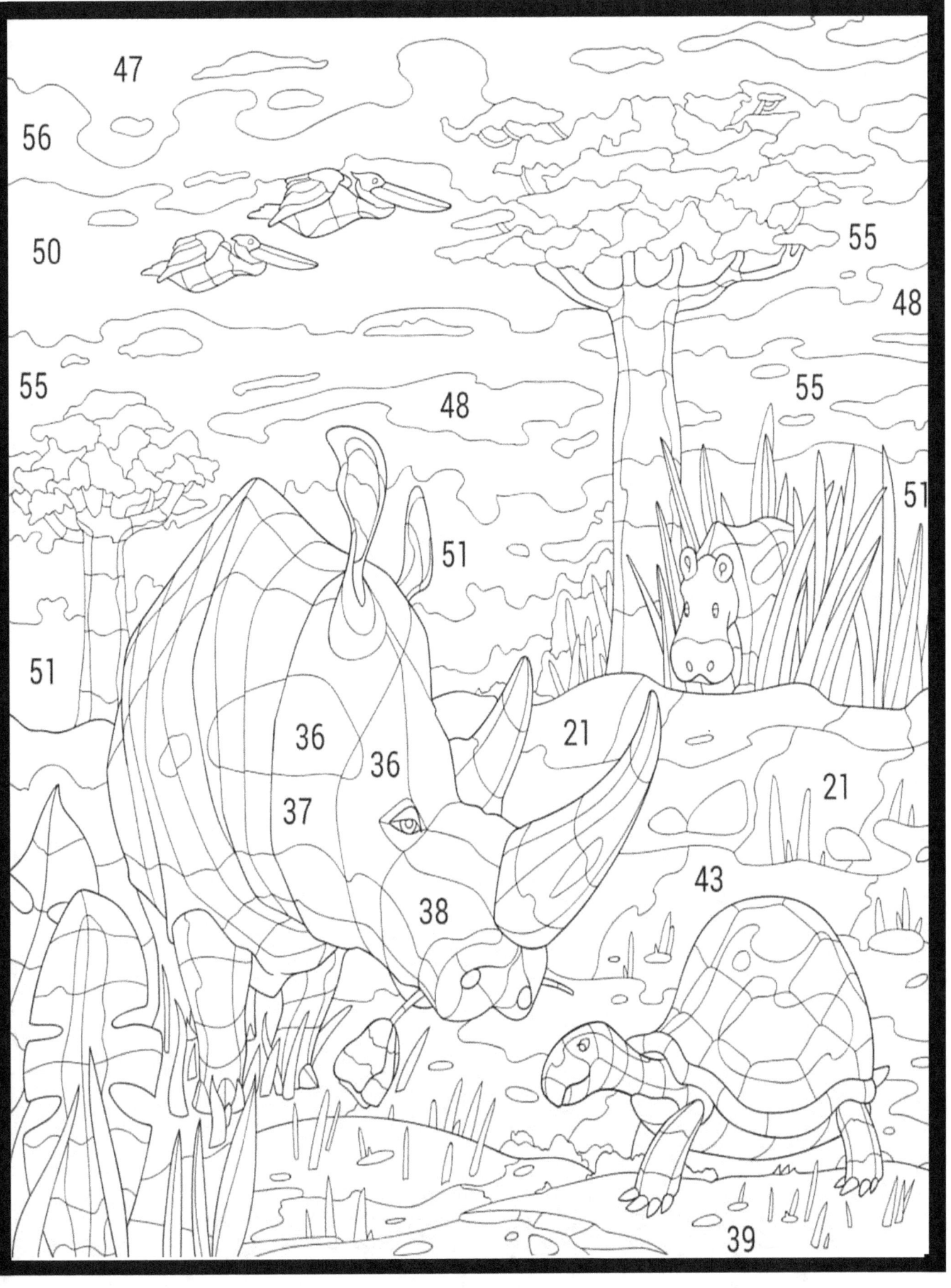

The Big Elephant

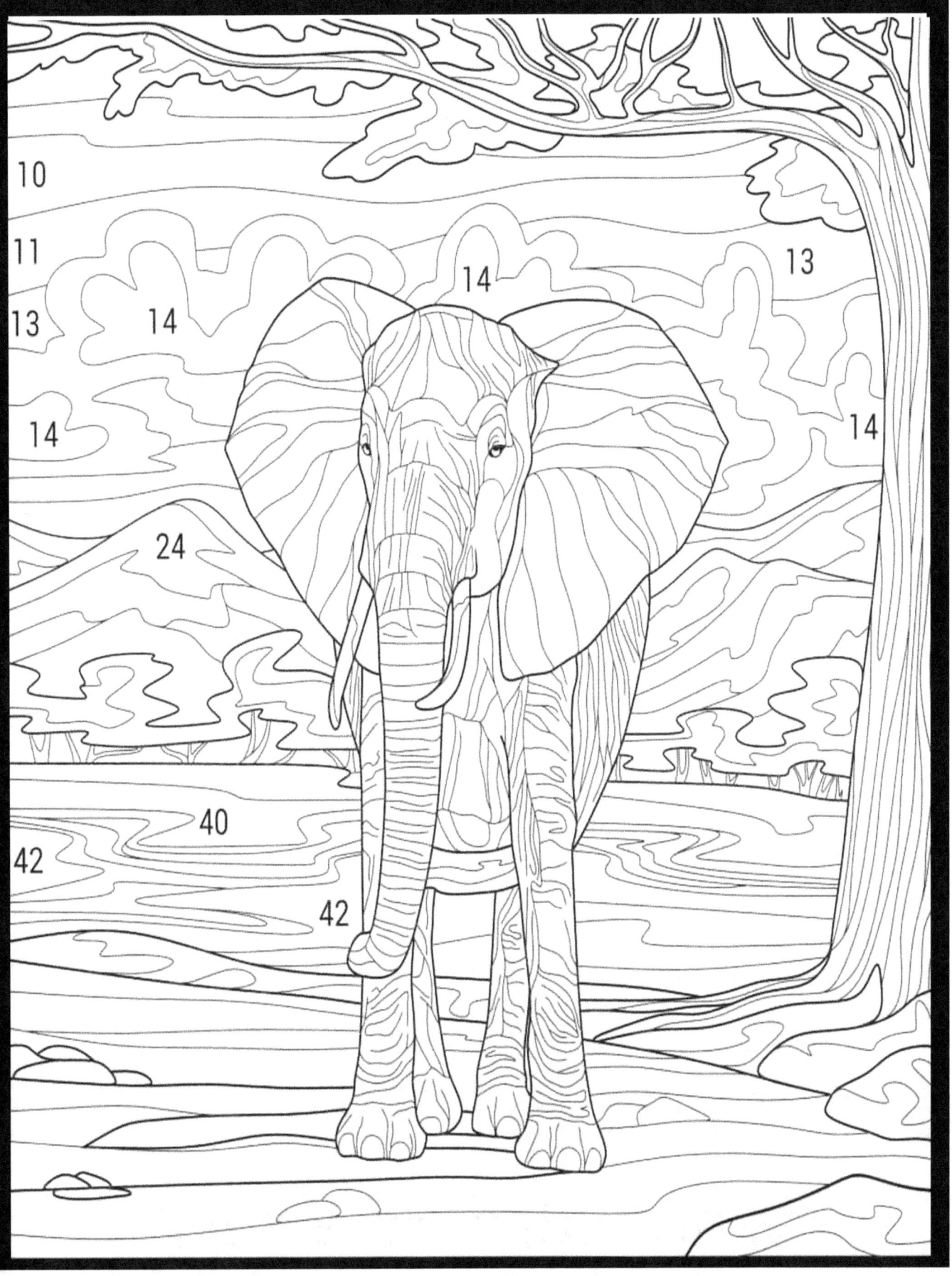

# What kind of Beer?

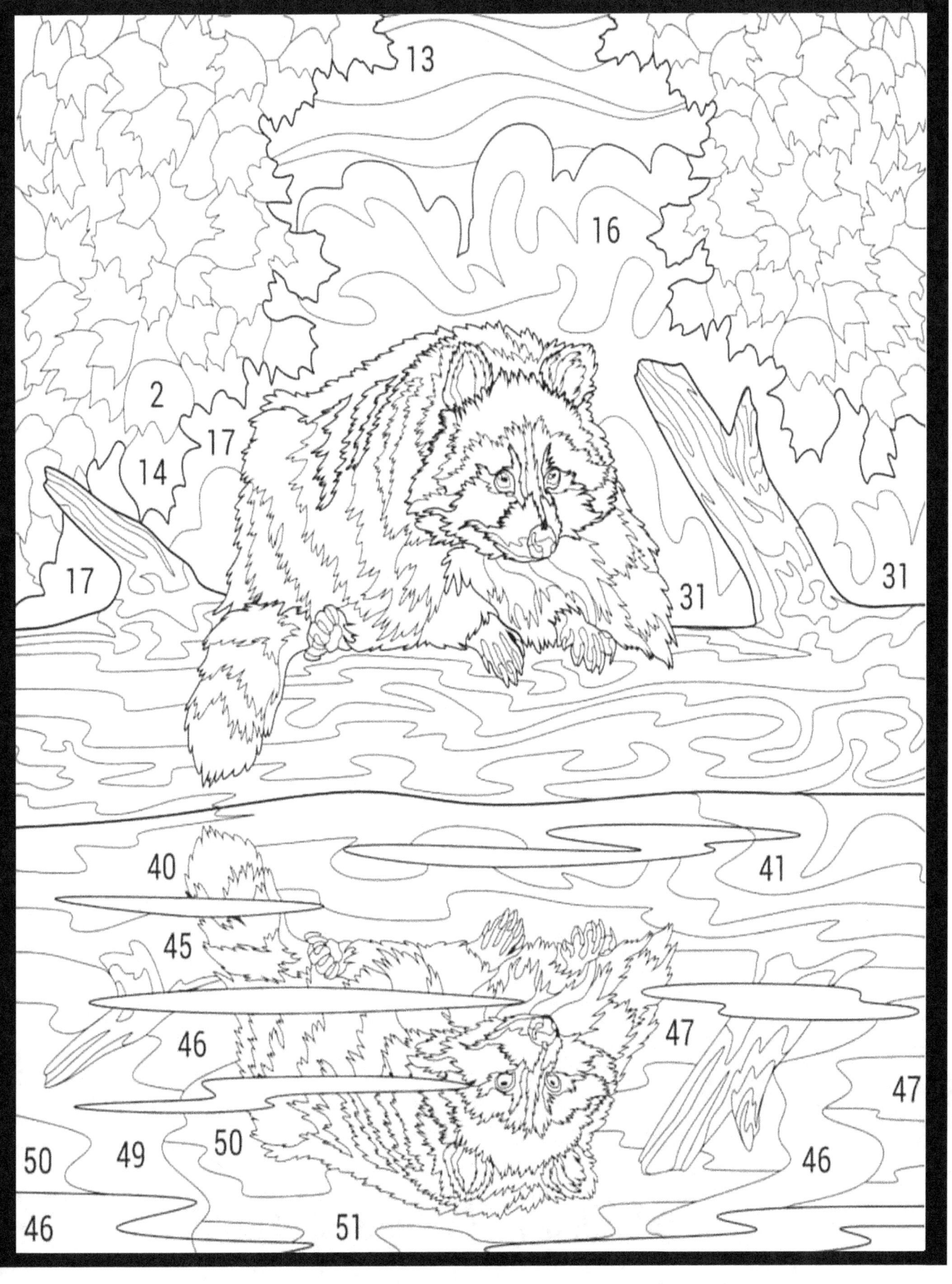

WILD HORSE

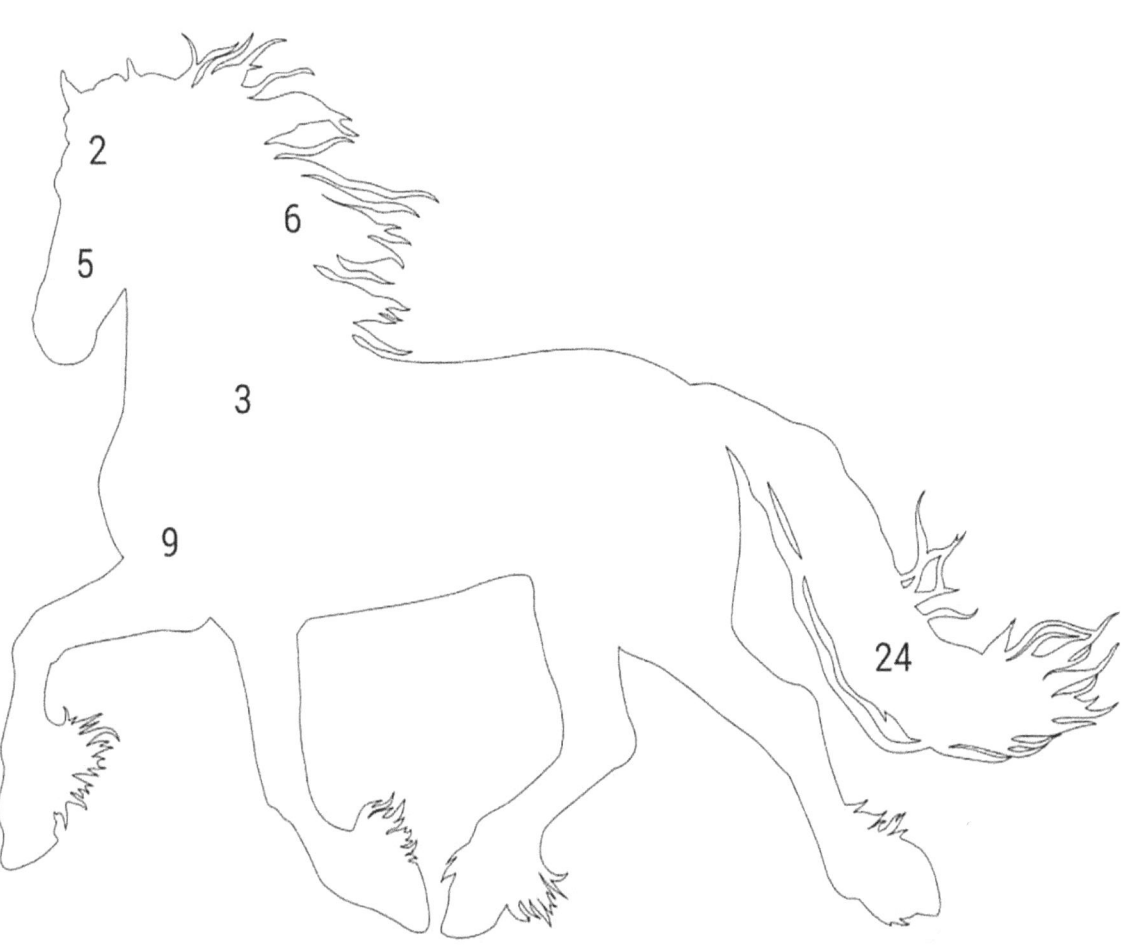

PREDATORY CAT

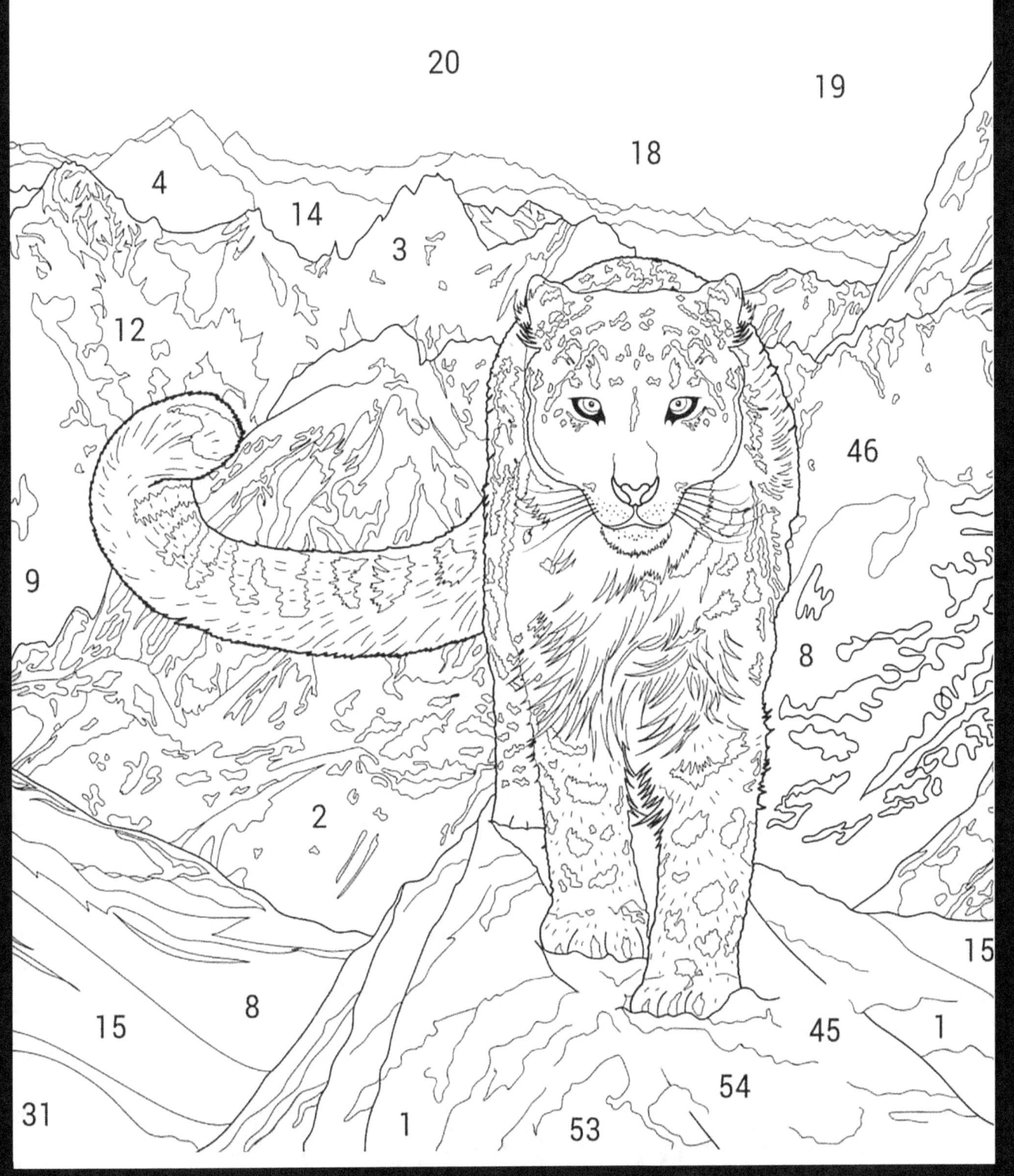

SEAL ANIMALS

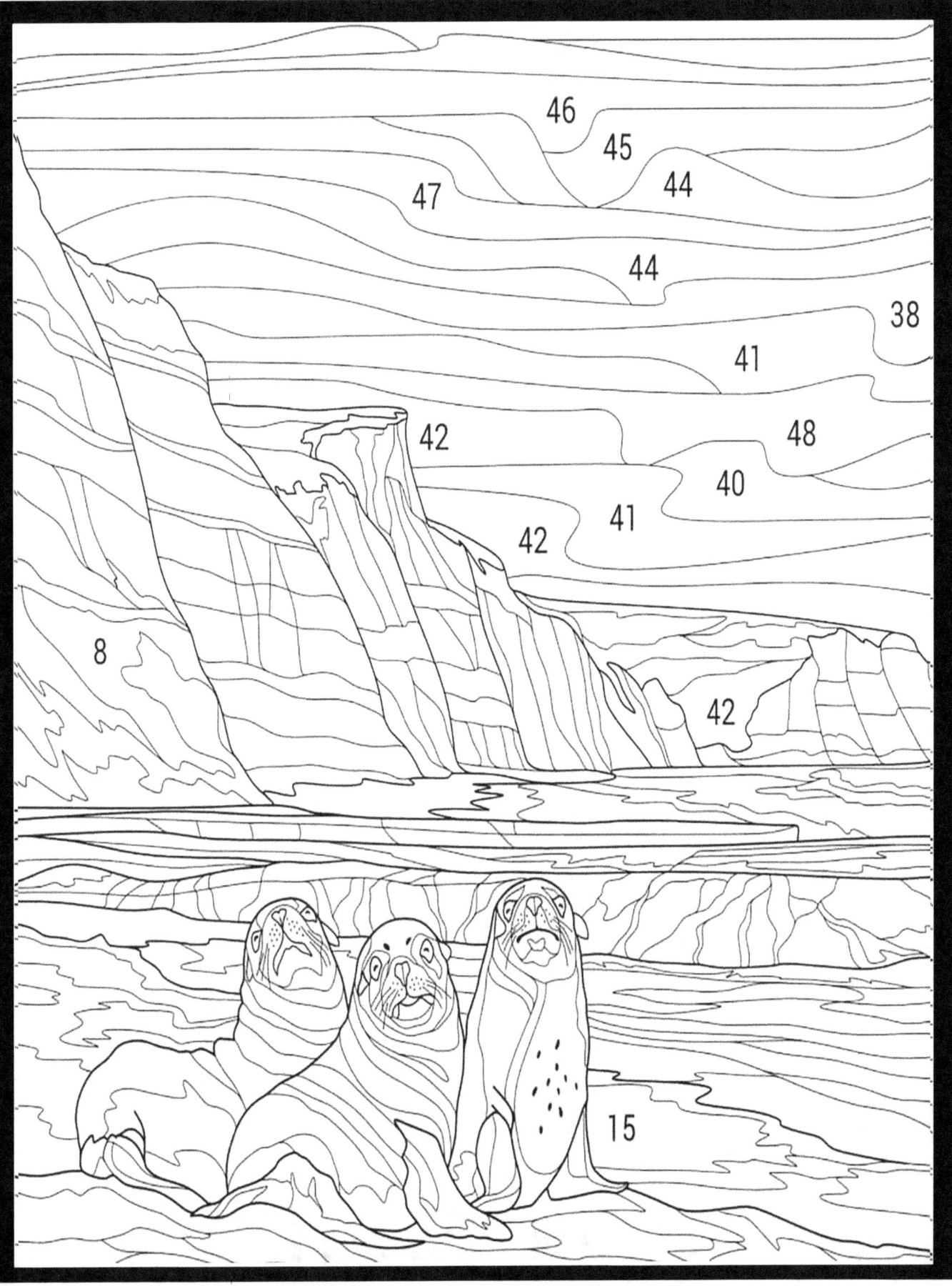

COW FLOCK

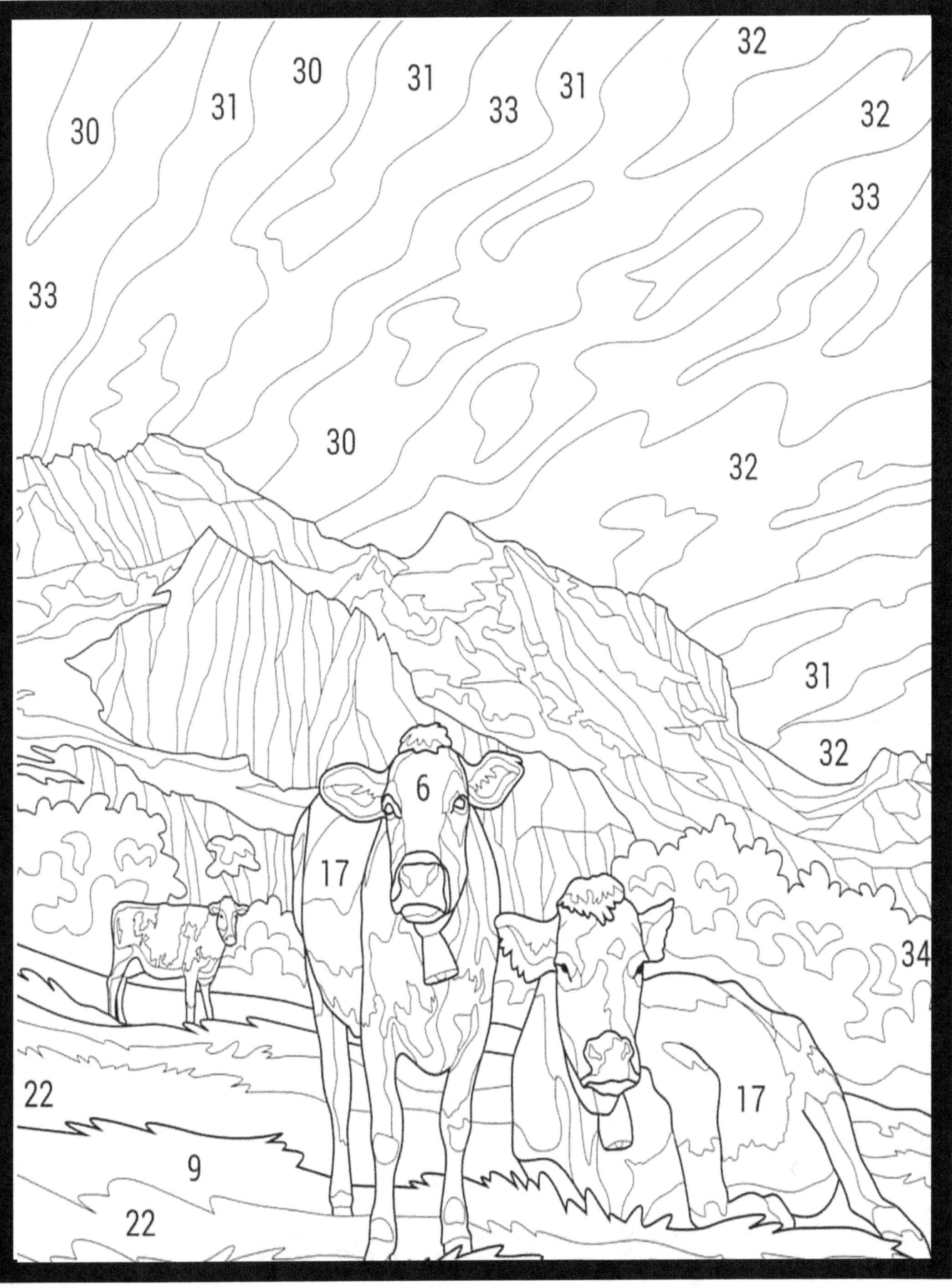

WILD RABBIT

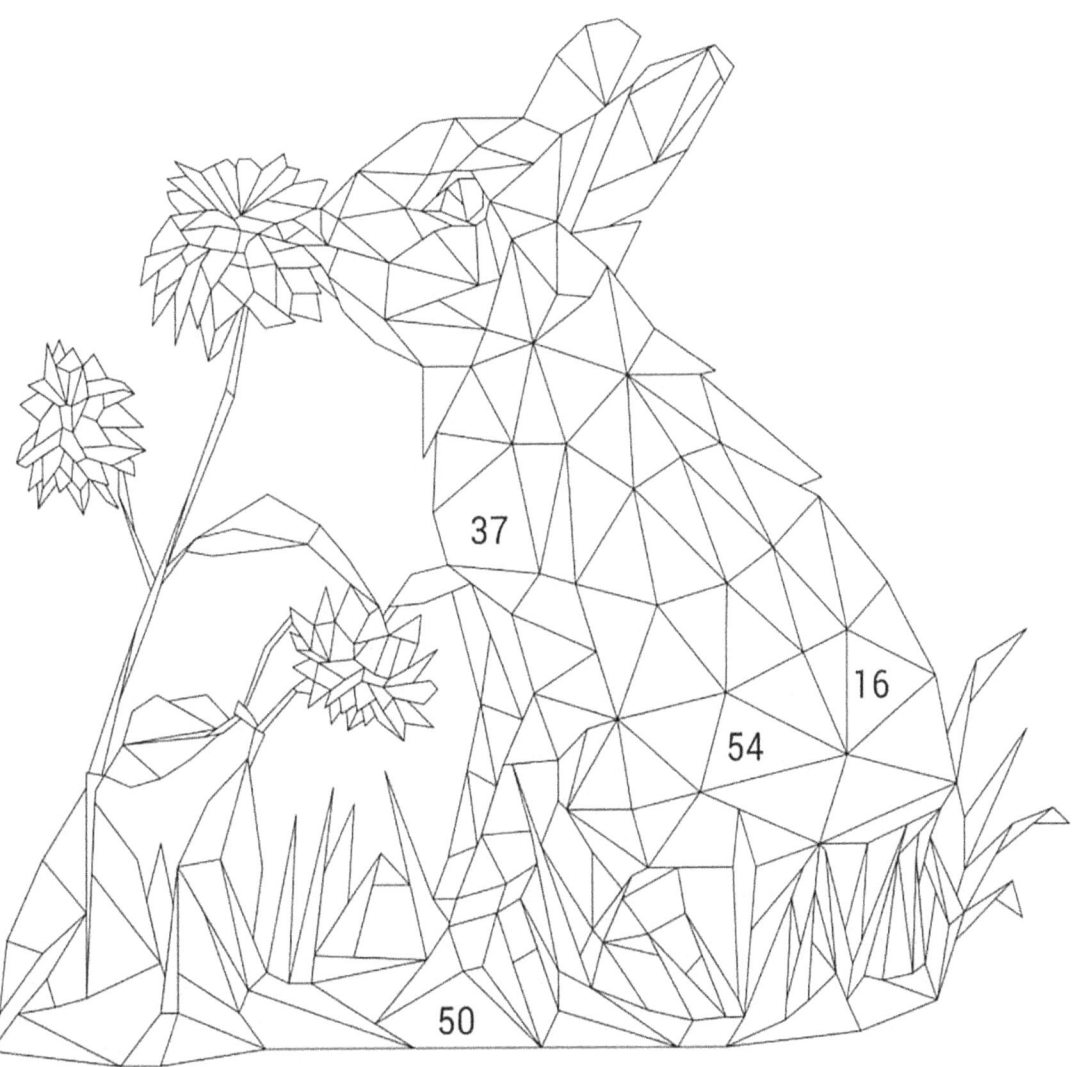

NICE DEER

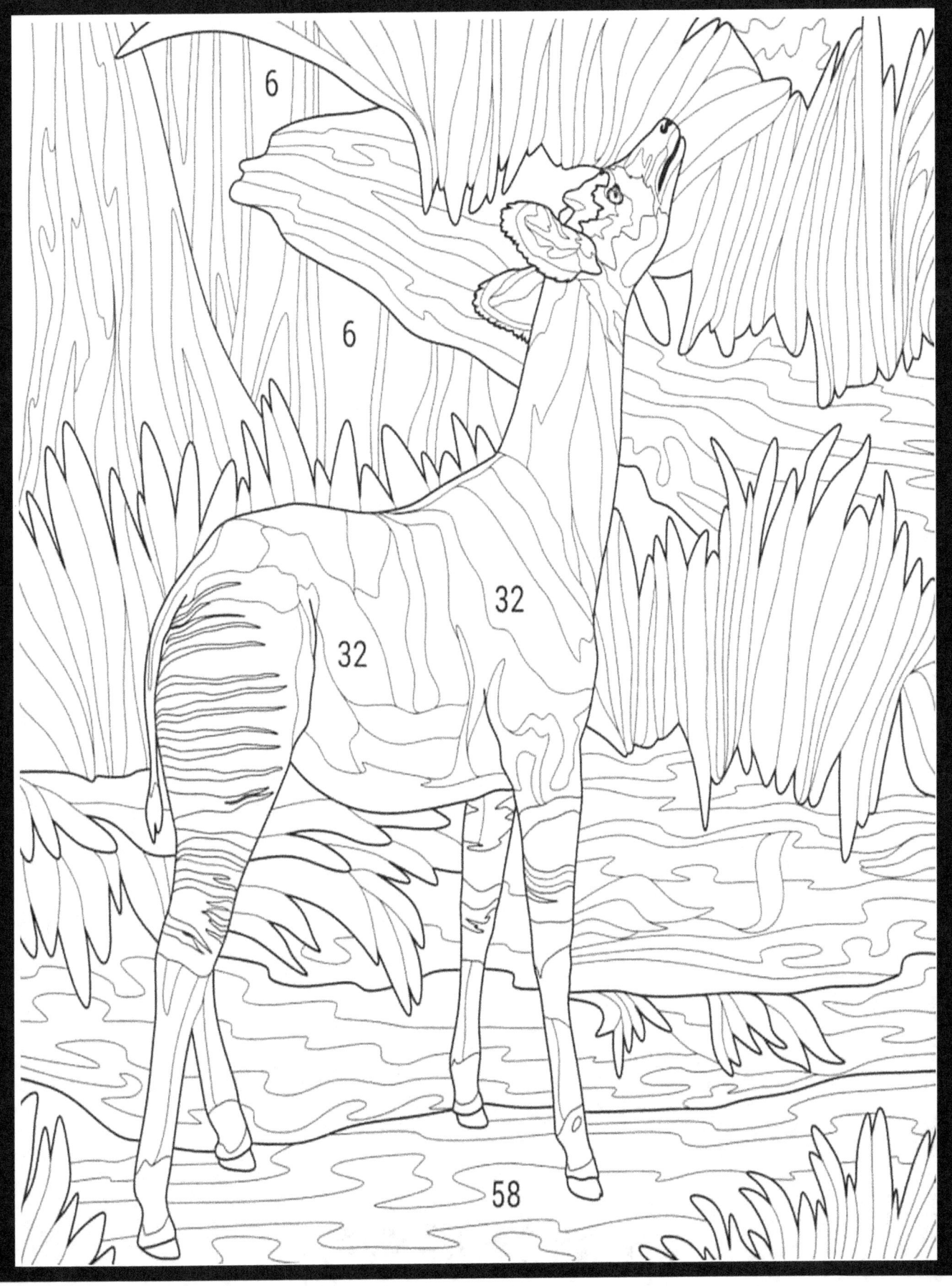

LIONESS

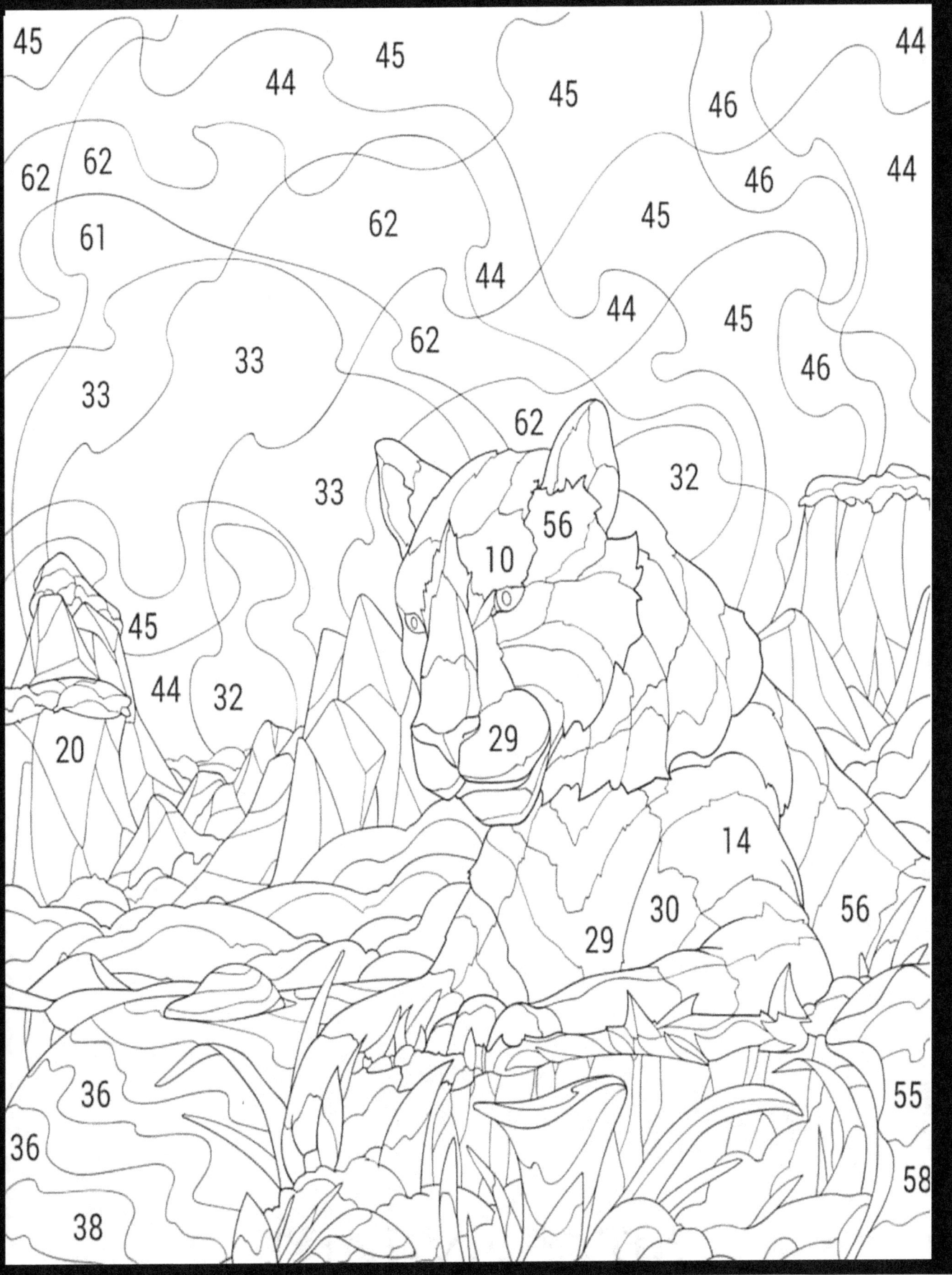

NICE DHABI

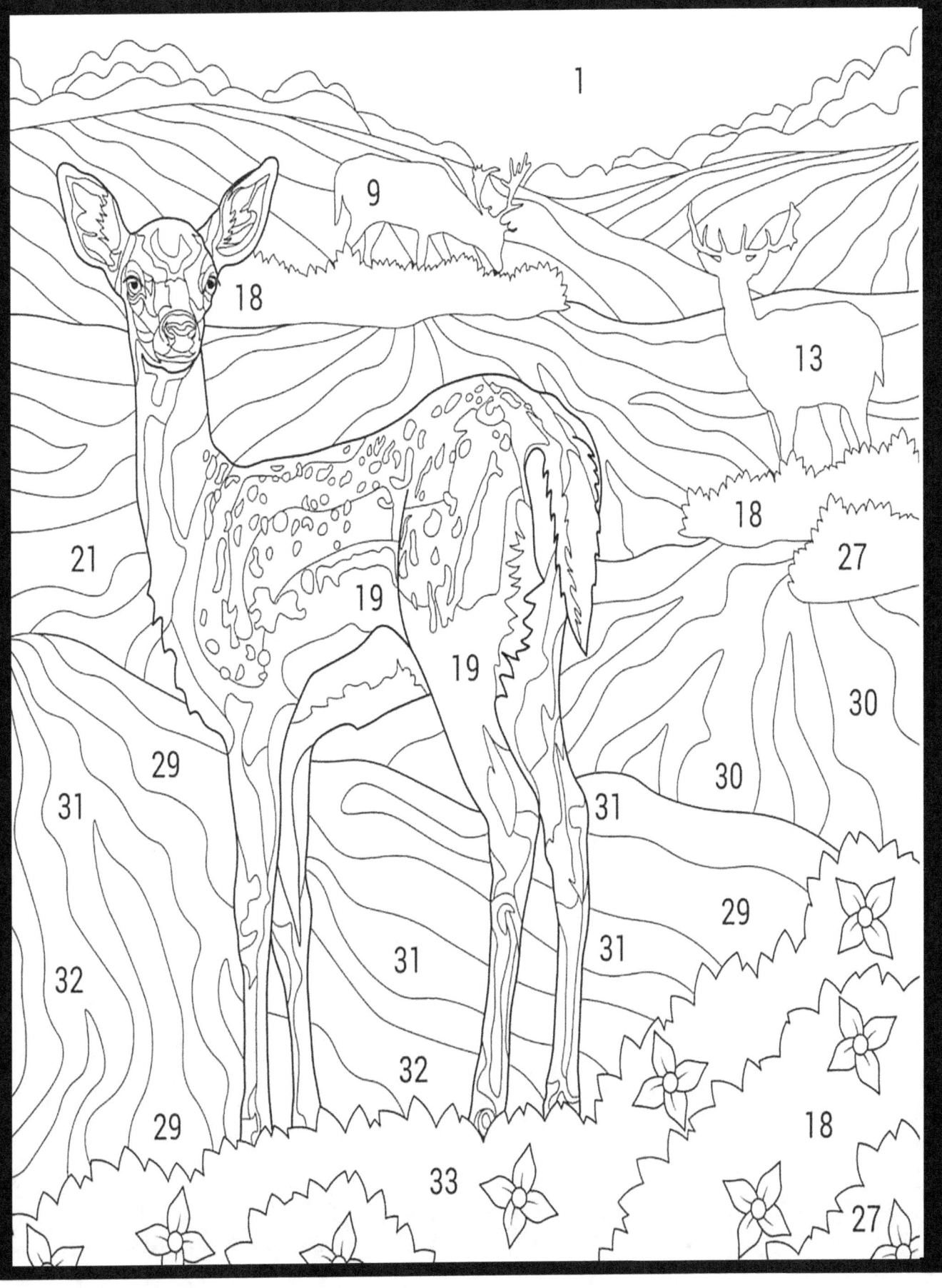

# ACTIVITY AND VITALITY

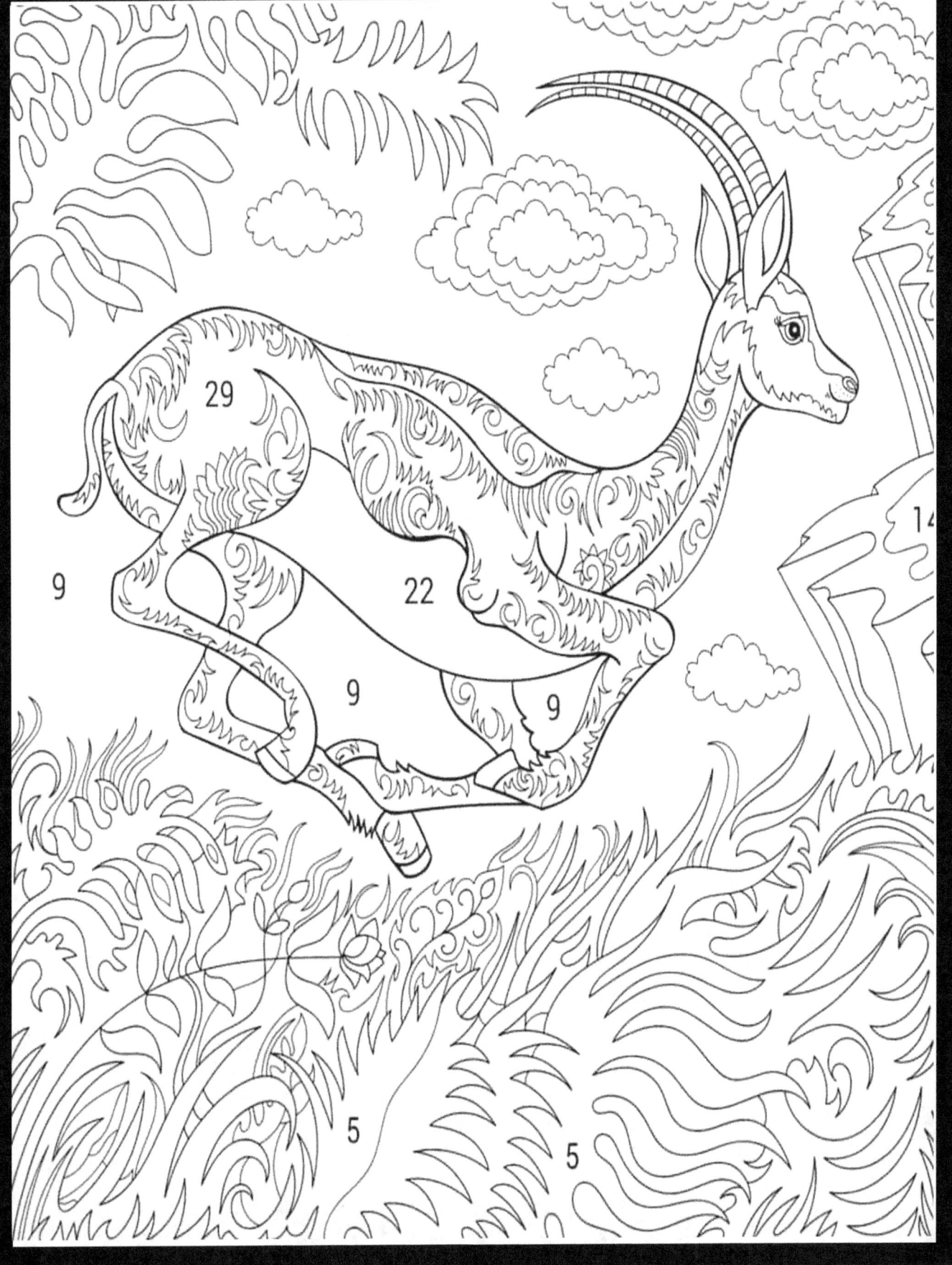

LAZY KOALA

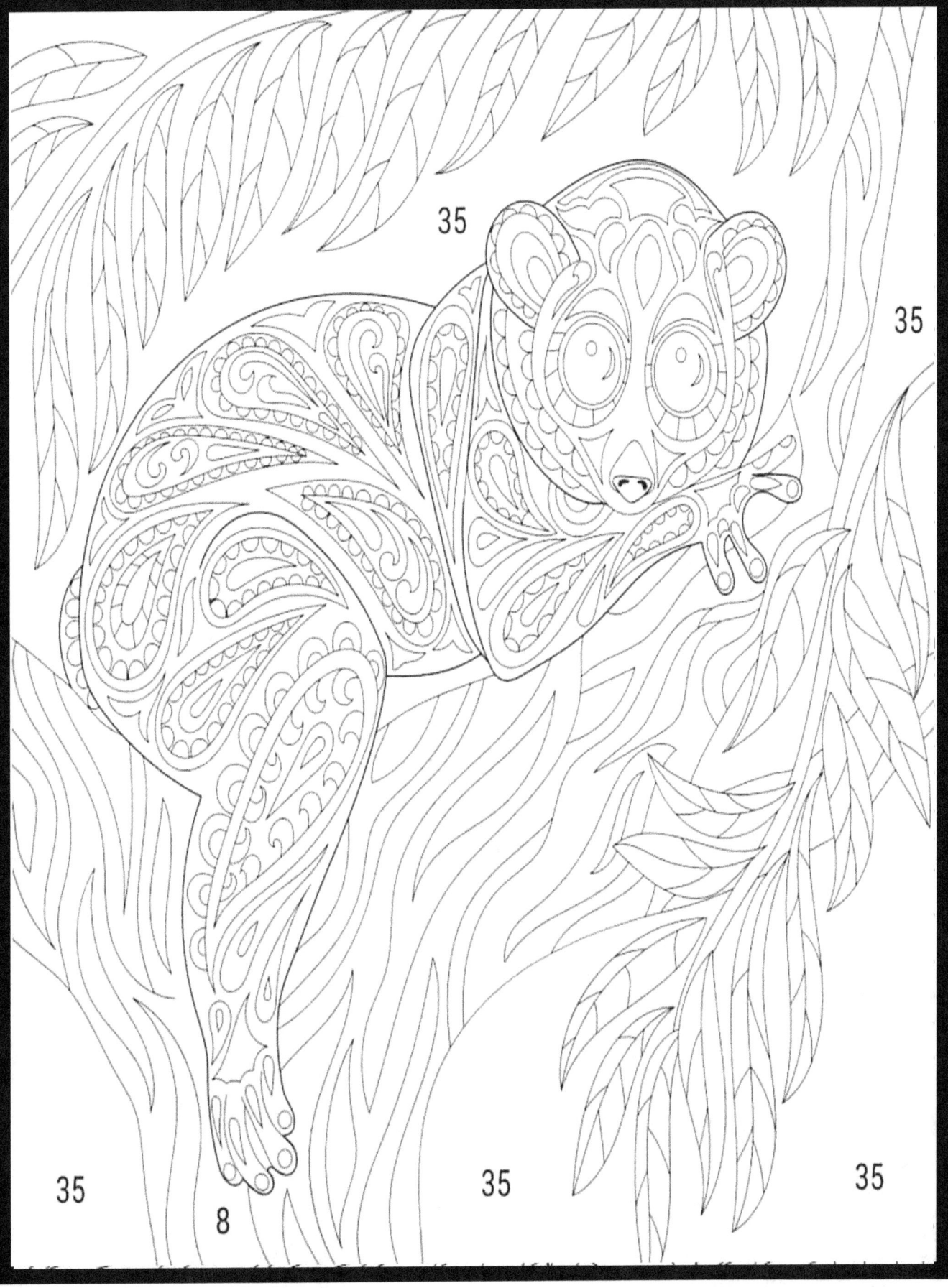